MY TONGUE IS THE PEN OF A READY WRITER

THERAPEUTIC THOUGHTS HEALING THE HEART

DE ANDREA DUDLEY

My Tongue is the Pen of a Ready Writer
by De Andrea Dudley
Copyright © 2020 De Andrea Dudley

ISBN # 978-1-63360-140-6

Unless otherwise noted, all scripture quotations taken from the Holy Bible, New International Version®, NIV®. Copyright © 1973, 1978, 1984, 2011 by Biblica, Inc.™ Used by permission of Zondervan. All rights reserved worldwide. www.zondervan.com The "NIV" and "New International Version" are trademarks registered in the United States Patent and Trademark Office by Biblica, Inc.

All rights reserved under International Copyright Law. Written permission must be secured from the publisher/author to reproduce, copy, or transmit any part of this book.

For Worldwide Distribution Printed in the U.S.A.

Urban Press
P.O. Box 8881
Pittsburgh, PA 15221-0881 USA
412.646.2780
www.urbanpress.us

INTRODUCTION

THROUGHOUT MY LIFE I HAVE NEVER BEEN MUCH OF A TALKER. I BEGAN TO EXPRESS MY LIFE WITH ALL ITS PAIN, JOY, SORROWS AND THINGS I KNEW TO BE TRUE AND EXPERIENCED THROUGH JOURNALING AND POETRY.
I WOULD RECITE MY POEMS IN CHURCH, BUT ONCE THEY WERE WRITTEN AND SPOKEN BEFORE THE CONGREGATION, THEY WERE QUICKLY FORGOTTEN, PUT AWAY, AND LOST, NEVER TO BE SEEN AGAIN.
THE WORDS WITHIN THIS BOOK WERE NOT CREATED JUST FOR THE PURPOSE OF RHYMING. MOST OF THE POEMS ARE BASED ON SOMETHING I'VE EXPERIENCED IN LIFE AND WENT ON TO OVERCOME IT.
PLACING MY JOURNEY IN BOOK FORM IS MY WAY OF HELPING SOMEBODY, FOLLOWING MY BELIEF THAT EACH ONE MUST REACH ONE.
THE TITLE I CHOSE FOR THIS BOOK DIDN'T HAPPEN BY CHANCE. THIS IS A VERSE FROM THE BIBLE FOUND IN PSALMS 45:1. ONE DAY WHILE SPENDING TIME WITH THE LORD IN PRAYER AND HIS WORD, I CAME ACROSS THIS VERSE AND I HAD WHAT SOME WOULD CALL "A LIGHTBULB MOMENT." I SAID TO THE LORD, "THIS IS EXACTLY WHAT IT FEELS LIKE WHEN I WRITE!"
THE BIBLE SPEAKS OF THE TONGUE AS A SMALL, BUT MIGHTY WEAPON. IN FACT, IT SAYS, DEATH AND LIFE ARE WITHIN THE POWER OF IT.
IF SOMETHING FROM ANY PAGE IN THIS BOOK CAUSES YOU, AS THE READER, TO TURN AWAY FROM SIN, GAIN INSIGHT, THINK BEFORE YOU DO SOMETHING, OR GIVES YOU VICTORY OVER EVEN ONE PROBLEM OR OBSTACLE IN YOUR LIFE, THEN I'VE SUCCEEDED AS A WRITER.

Reflection 1

I HAVE BEEN WRITING POETRY FOR A LONG TIME WITH NO PLANS OF DOING ANYTHING WITH IT BESIDES RECITING. ONCE I DECIDED TO TRANSFORM THESE BEAUTIFUL WORDS INTO A BOOK, I NEEDED TO FIGURE OUT WHAT THE TITLE WOULD BE.

WHO KNEW I'D FIND MY ANSWER IN THE WORD? ONE DAY, JUST READING THE BOOK OF PSALMS, THESE WORDS JUMPED OFF THE PAGE: "MY TONGUE IS THE PEN OF A READY WRITER." I KNEW RIGHT THEN AND THERE WHAT MY TITLE SHOULD BE. THIS IS A PERFECT DESCRIPTION OF A POET WHO IS ALWAYS THINKING AND THEN SEEING POETRY IN SOME SHAPE OR FORM. WE COULD BE WATCHING A CHILD PLAYING OR A FLOWER BLOOMING; IT DOESN'T MATTER. EVERYTHING IS SUBJECT TO A DEEPER REVELATION.

PSALM 45:1

"MY HEART IS OVERFLOWING WITH A GOOD THEME
I RECITE MY COMPOSITION CONCERNING THE KING
MY TONGUE IS THE PEN OF A READY WRITER."

THIS WAS A GIFT THAT I'VE NEVER CONSIDERED AS ONE,
ONLY SOMETHING I WOULD DO FOR FUN—
IN MY SPARE TIME TRYING TO UNWIND,
PERSONAL THERAPY TO SET FREE THE TROUBLES DEEP WITHIN ME.

COME TO FIND OUT MY MOM DID THE SAME
TO EASE HER PAIN.
WHAT AN INSPIRATION!
THIS THING GOES FROM GENERATION TO GENERATION.

I WOULD ALWAYS WRITE
AND THIS WAS MY WAY OF PUTTING UP A FIGHT,
BREAKING THE SILENCE
WITHOUT THE VIOLENCE.

GOD KNEW THIS WOULD BE MY WAY OF GETTING THINGS OUT,
NO WORRIES, NO DOUBTS.
NO ONE COULD CRITICIZE AND NO ONE COULD JUDGE;
JUST BETWEEN ME, MY PEN, AND PAPER.

IF MY MIND CHANGED, I COULD WRITE IT DOWN LATER.
NO MORE HIDING; SEEN BUT NOT HEARD IS A MYTH
HE GAVE ME THIS GIFT;
THE WORDS I SPEAK HIS PEOPLE WILL LIFT.

THEY GIVE CREDIT TO ME, BUT I CONTINUE TO LINGER
UNTIL CHRIST FLOWS THROUGH THESE FINGERS—
HE WHO HELPS ME TO SPEAK MY LIFE.
TELL MY STORY SO ONLY HE GETS THE GLORY
EVERY PRAYER YOU'VE HEARD AS I DELIVER YOUR SPOKEN WORD.

Reflection 2

THIS POEM IS THE ONLY ONE I HAVEN'T HAD A PERSONAL EXPERIENCE WITH.

I HAVE HAD OPPORTUNITIES TO SPEAK BEFORE THE CONGREGATION IN A TIME WE REFER TO AS "WHAT THE LORD IS SAYING TO ME." THIS GIVES CONGREGANTS A PLATFORM TO SHARE WHAT'S GOING ON IN THEIR LIVES AS CHRISTIANS AND HOW THEY ARE GROWING SPIRITUALLY BECAUSE GOD IS NOT JUST TALKING TO THE PASTOR, BUT TO EVERYONE. ARE WE LISTENING?
I AM NO LONGER THE ONE TO SAY, "I'LL NEVER DO THIS OR THAT" BECAUSE THE LORD HAS PROVEN ME WRONG AT THIS STAGE IN MY LIFE. I DON'T WANT TO STUNT MY GROWTH BECAUSE OF UNFAMILIAR TERRITORY. I DO KNOW THAT I HAVE BEEN SET APART FROM CHILDHOOD AND ONE DAY I HAD A DREAM. IN THE DREAM, I SAT IN MY COURTYARD AND JESUS CAME TOWARD ME. EVEN THOUGH I WAS A LITTLE GIRL, I KNEW IT WAS JESUS. HE TOLD ME, "I WILL NEVER LEAVE YOU." I TELL YOU THAT HE HAS KEPT HIS PROMISE. THOUGH I HAVE NOT HAD ANY EXPERIENCE AS A PASTOR, I DO BELIEVE THE LORD GIVES PASTORS A UNIQUE HEART FOR HIS PEOPLE AND I HAVE ATTEMPTED TO DESCRIBE IT IN THIS POEM.

THE HEART OF A PASTOR

AS A CHILD, I KNEW I WAS SET APART
TO GROW INTO A WOMAN AFTER GOD'S OWN HEART,
ANOINTED TO PREACH THE GOSPEL TO THE PROUD AND LAWFUL.

HE HAS SENT ME TO HEAL
THE BROKENHEARTED AND PREACH DELIVERANCE TO THE CAPTIVES,
BUT THIS IS WHERE IT BECOMES UNATTRACTIVE.

"HOW CAN SHE PREACH DELIVERANCE
WHEN SHE'S NEVER TASTED OF MY SIN?
SHE WOULDN'T EVEN KNOW WHERE TO BEGIN."

CAN'T YOU SEE IT'S NOT ME, BUT
GOD GIVES THE ABILITY TO TAP INTO THE VERY STRUGGLES OF YOU?
IT MAKES IT SEEM AS THOUGH THIS IS SOMETHING I'VE BEEN THROUGH—
NOT IN THE NATURAL, BUT THE SPIRITUAL.

GETTING RID OF OLD MINDSETS AND RITUALS,
HE HAS HELPED ME TO GIVE THE RECOVERY OF SIGHT TO THE BLIND,
SET AT LIBERTY THOSE WHO ARE BRUISED—
THE PEOPLE NOT EASILY SOOTHED.

I HAVE TO TRUST GOD TO USE ME
AND CUT THROUGH YEARS OF MISERY AND EVERY STRONGHOLD—
FOR THIS I MUST BE BOLD.

THE PEOPLE YOU'VE CALLED ME TO I CAN'T LEAD ASTRAY.
SOMETIMES THEY'RE NICE AND SOMETIMES THEY ATTACK,
BECAUSE OF THE ANOINTING THIS IS WHAT I ATTRACT.

THE PRICE, MAKE SURE I CAN AFFORD,
I PRESS AND PRESS UNTIL I'M PRESSED OUT OF MEASURE.
MY HEART IS NEAR MY TREASURE;
I WILL GET MY REWARD,
FOR I HAVE PREACHED THE ACCEPTABLE YEAR OF THE LORD.

Reflection 3

SOMETIMES WE GO THROUGH TRIALS AND TRIBULATIONS AND FEEL LIKE THINGS WILL NEVER GET BETTER. LIFE CAN BE SO DIFFICULT AND IT SEEMS LIKE EVERYWHERE WE TURN, THERE'S TROUBLE.

NOBODY KNOWS WHAT WE'VE ENDURED.

NOBODY UNDERSTANDS WHAT WE'RE GOING THROUGH—OR SO IT SEEMS.

LISTEN, YOU ARE NOT THE ONLY ONE FACING PROBLEMS AND HARDSHIPS. YOU ARE NOT ALONE IN THIS FIGHT.

ONE DAY THE SUN IS GOING TO SHINE AGAIN AND WHEN IT DOES, YOU WILL BE A LIVING TESTIMONY TO SOMEONE. YOUR STRUGGLE TODAY WILL SOON BE SOMEBODY'S WAY OF ESCAPE TOMORROW, BUT WHEN YOU'RE IN THE MIDST OF IT, YOU DON'T CARE ABOUT BEING A WITNESS. YOU ARE JUST TRYING TO MAKE IT OUT ALIVE.

JUST KNOW GOD'S GOT YOUR BACK AND IT'S GOING TO BE ALRIGHT.

I GOT A FEELIN'

I GOT A FEELIN' EVERYTHING'S GONNA BE ALRIGHT—
MAYBE NOT TONIGHT,
BUT ONE DAY THE SON'S GONNA SHINE BRIGHT IN MY LIFE.

NOT SPEAKING OF THE SUN IN THE SKY,
BUT OF THE ONE WHO HAD TO DIE FOR YOU AND I.
HE'S GONNA PURGE ME, HELP ME BE
WHO I NEED TO BE FOR MYSELF AND MY FAMILY.

ALWAYS DOING WHAT'S RIGHT CAN AT TIMES BE A FIGHT.
GETTING DISCOURAGED
AS I LOSE MY FOOTAGE,
BUT I GOT A FEELIN' EVERYTHING'S GONNA BE ALRIGHT—
MAYBE NOT TONIGHT.

BUT WHO'S TO SAY
WHEN THE LORD WILL MAKE A WAY?
OPEN UP THE GATES AND I NO LONGER GO ASTRAY,
OR HAVE TO WAIT TO BE HEALED.

THE LORD WILL REVEAL THE REAL ME,
NOT THE ONE I'M TRYING TO BE.
SHE HAS THE POTENTIAL TO GROW
BEYOND WHAT I REALLY KNOW.

SOMEWHERE DOWN DEEP WHERE THE ENEMY
CAN'T REACH, WHERE HE'S NOT EVEN PERMITTED TO TROD—
ONLY ME AND GOD.

WE GOT WORK TO DO; CAN'T STOP UNTIL HE'S THROUGH.
IN THIS RACE I EMBARK,
I HAVE TO PRESS TOWARD THE MARK.
WHEN I FEEL I CAN NO LONGER RUN,
THERE'S STILL MAJOR WORK TO BE DONE.

THE MOUNTAIN'S INSURMOUNTABLE
WHAT MORE CAN I DO? WHICH WAY DO I GO?
DON'T MOVE TOO FAST OR TOO SLOW.

LORD, HERE COMES THAT SAME TEST,
BUT THIS TIME THE ARMOR'S COVERING MY CHEST.
ONE, TWO, THREE, POW!
AIN'T NO STOPPIN' ME NOW.

I FIGHT TO THE FINISH; WE BOTH GO DOWN.
ONE IS DESTROYED, THE OTHER HEAVEN BOUND.
I'M IN IT TO WIN IT, MY PRIZE THE CROWN.

I GOT A FEELIN' EVERYTHING'S GONNA BE ALRIGHT—
MAYBE NOT TONIGHT,
BUT JUST YOU WAIT AND SEE.
THE LORD'S GONNA REVEAL A NEW ME.

READ IN BETWEEN LINES,
MY LIGHT HAS TO SHINE SO GOD CAN BE GLORIFIED.
CAN'T HIDE ANYMORE, HE'S PUSHING ME TO THE FRONT LINE—
AND MY GIFTS HAVE MADE ROOM.
HE'S CALLED FORTH MY LAZARUS OUT OF THE TOMB

I'M SHINING SO BRIGHT CAUSE NOW I KNOW
EVERYTHING'S GONNA BE ALRIGHT

Reflection 4

NO MATTER WHAT STRUGGLES WE FACE, WHEN GOD SAYS HE HAS OUR BACK, HE REALLY DOES. OUR PROBLEMS MAY SEEM LIKE THEY WILL NEVER CEASE. IT'S A MOUNTAIN WE CAN'T CLIMB OR A VALLEY WE CAN'T CROSS.
SOMETIMES SITUATIONS WILL HAVE US WONDERING WHERE GOD IS. WE HAVE PEOPLE SITTING, WATCHING, AND WAITING FOR OUR DOWNFALL. WHY AREN'T THEY PRAYING? WHY DO THEY WANT TO SEE YOU FAIL? DO THEY ENVY SOMETHING YOU DON'T EVEN KNOW YOU POSSESS? THE STRUGGLES, ALONG WITH THE PERSECUTION, ARE REAL. THE PEACE THROUGH ALL THIS FRUSTRATION IS THAT GOD SEES AND KNOWS WHAT WE ARE GOING THROUGH. HE WILL AVENGE US. HE WILL FIGHT OUR BATTLES. GOD TAKES CARE OF HIS OWN.

I AM THE GREATEST

AS I LOOK BACK OVER MY LIFE,
I FIND MYSELF THINKING LIKE, "WAS IT WORTH IT?"
I SAY, "YES", BUT I WAS STILL KICKIN' AND SCREAMIN',
GOIN' THROUGH THE TRIALS AND TESTS
CREATED FROM MY OWN MESS.

A PATH I DIDN'T WANT TO TAKE,
NOT EVEN FOR RIGHTEOUSNESS SAKE.
BETWEEN A ROCK AND A HARD PLACE, I DID NOT BELONG.
LIKE THE PRODIGAL SON, I HAD TO COME HOME.

MY WORLD CRUMBLING ALL AROUND ME
AT THE TIME I DIDN'T KNOW WHAT TO DO—WOULD YOU?

THERE'S NO TIME LIKE THE PRESENT
TO LEARN FROM YOUR MISTAKES.
REPENT AND TURN BEFORE IT'S TOO LATE.

TORMENTED BY MY CHOICES,
I FELT ALL HOPE WAS LOST.
I KEPT MYSELF IN PRISON
AND WOULDN'T ALLOW MYSELF TO BE FREE.

JESUS WAS MY ANSWER,
BUT CONDEMNATION THREW AWAY THE KEY.
I WOULD COME TO CHURCH HALF-DEAD,
GOING THROUGH UNNECESSARY SUFFERING,
BUT STILL UNDER HIS COVERING.

REMOVE THE SCALES FROM MY EYES,
FOR I AM NOT GREATER
THAN MY CREATOR.
YOU KNOCK AT MY DOOR AND SAY,
"GO AND SIN NO MORE!"

THE DEVIL THOUGHT HE HAD ME,
BUT GOD MADE HIM LET ME GO.
THREW SOME SERIOUS BLOWS
WHEN I STEPPED OUTSIDE THE DOOR GOD CLOSED.
I WAS DOWN FOR THE COUNT—ONE, TWO, THREE!

BLOOD COVERED MY EYES,
BUT GOD SAID, "VICTORY YOU SHALL SEE!"
WHOSE REPORT WILL YOU BELIEVE
WHEN TROUBLE HAS BROUGHT YOU TO YOUR KNEES?
BEGGING IT TO STOP!

READY TO SURRENDER TO YOUR CONTENDER,
GOD SAYS "GET UP, 'CAUSE I'M ABOUT TO STRUT MY STUFF!
WATCH MY FANCY FOOTWORK, THE DEVIL HASN'T HAD ENOUGH!

"DID YOU FORGET THE BATTLE'S NOT YOURS, BUT THE LORD'S?
MOVE OUT THE WAY AND I WILL REPAY,
FOR HE TRIED TO DESTROY WHAT'S MINE!
NOW IT'S TIME!

"I AM GOD AND GOD ALONE
ONE SHOT TO THE DOME; HE'S DONE.
I'M THE ONE, THE AUTHOR AND FINISHER;
THERE'S ONLY ONE WINNER—ME!

"I AM THE BEGINNING AND THE END,
I AM HE WHO IS WITHOUT SIN!
I AM THE ALPHA AND OMEGA,
THE CREATOR—THERE IS NO ONE GREATER!"

Reflection 5

THERE WAS A TIME IN HISTORY WHEN BEFORE THERE WAS AN ACTUAL BATTLE, THERE WAS A SOUND THAT PRECEDED IT. MOST OF THE TIME IT WAS THE BEAT OF THE DRUMS. WHEN ARMIES HEARD IT, THEY KNEW IT WAS TIME TO GET READY: "THIS MEANS WAR!" IT WAS A TIME TO DROP THEIR REGULARLY SCHEDULED PROGRAM AND PUT THE TRIBAL PAINT ON THEIR FACES BECAUSE IT WAS ABOUT TO GO DOWN.

WHILE YOU ARE IN THE FIGHT, IT IS NOT THE TIME TO COWER UNDER PRESSURE. YOU HAVE TO PUT ON THAT ARMOR AND GO IN WITH THE MINDSET OF "LOSING IS NOT AN OPTION." LISTEN AND FOLLOW THE INSTRUCTIONS OF YOUR COMMANDER-IN-CHIEF. BE THE FRONTLINE SOLDIER HE CALLED YOU TO BE AND DON'T BACK DOWN OR OUT.

WAR CRY

THERE'S A SOUND IN MY EAR THAT'S BECOMING VERY CLEAR.
DO YOU HEAR WHAT I HEAR?

WHAT IS GOD TRYING TO TELL YOU?
LIFT YOUR HANDS IN THE AIR
DO YOU HEAR WHAT I HEAR?

NEW LEVELS COMING TO YOU.
LIFT YOUR FEET OFF THE GROUND.
LISTEN TO THE SOUND,
THE SOUND OF ARMIES MARCHING IN WAR—
STANDING AT ATTENTION WAITING FOR DIRECTION.
MOVE LEFT, MOVE RIGHT,
PREPARE TO FIGHT!
NO COWARD SOLDIERS,
ONLY THE MILITANTS AND RADICALS.
PREPARE FOR BATTLE,
TAKE NO SABBATICALS.
DO YOU HEAR WHAT I HEAR?

TIME FOR WAR,
SHARPEN YOUR WEAPONS
IN PREPARATION,
NO TIME FOR FEAR.
DO YOU HEAR WHAT I HEAR?

Reflection 6

WE GO THROUGH LIFE EXPECTING NOT TO SUFFER ANYTHING, ESPECIALLY IF WE ARE CHRISTIANS. FOR WHATEVER REASON, WE FEEL THAT BECAUSE WE ARE CHILDREN OF GOD, SUFFERING SHOULD NOT BE NAMED AMONG US. WE FEEL LIKE WE SHOULD ONLY BE RECEIVING BLESSINGS.
THE WORD DOES DECLARE US BLESSED, BUT IT NEVER SAID WE WOULD NOT SUFFER ANY HEARTACHE, PAIN, SETBACKS, OR LOSSES. AS A MATTER OF FACT, IT SAYS THE CONTRARY. IN GOD'S WORD, WE WILL FIND HIM SAYING THINGS LIKE, "DENY YOURSELF, PICK UP YOUR CROSS, AND FOLLOW ME." "IF YOU SUFFER WITH ME, SO SHALL YOU REIGN," AND ON AND ON. HE TEACHES US TO EXPECT SUFFERING BECAUSE HE SUFFERED, AND WE WILL ALSO IF WE WANT TO BE IDENTIFIED AS BELONGING TO HIM.

SUFFERING

SUFFERING, OH SUFFERING, YOU'VE BEEN GIVEN A BAD NAME.
NOBODY WANTS YOU, BUT TO HAVE YOU IS GREAT GAIN.
CHRIST SAID IF I SUFFER, I'LL REIGN, BUT MY FLESH HAS ANOTHER PLAN,
JUST WANTING TO EAT THE GOOD OF THE LAND.

NOT TRYIN' TO BE PHONY,
BUT MY TRIALS MAKE ME FEEL LIKE A "ONE AND ONLY."
STRUGGLIN' TO KEEP MY TESTIMONY
THROUGH CONTINUAL HEARTACHE AND PAIN,
FORGETTING THERE WERE THOSE WHO HAVE GONE AHEAD
AND WERE LEFT FOR DEAD—STRUGGLING FOR BREATH.
AND GOD SAID, "GET UP, YOU HAVE NOT YET SUFFERED UNTO DEATH!"

WE ARE FOLLOWERS OF CHRIST, OR SO WE CLAIM.
WELL, LET ME TAKE YOU DOWN MEMORY LANE.
CLOSE YOUR EYES AND NOW IT'S YOU THAT DIES
ON A CROSS TO SAVE THE LOST.
DON'T HOLD YOUR BREATH; SUFFER 'TIL THERE'S NOTHING LEFT OF YOU.

FATHER, FORGIVE THEM FOR THEY KNOW NOT WHAT THEY DO!
IT IS FINISHED—NO SPOT, NO BLEMISH.
OPEN YOUR EYES; IT'S YOU NOW REVIVED AND RENEWED,
HAVING PAID THE PRICE FROM DEATH TO LIFE.

HAVING BEEN REJECTED, JESUS IS NOW REFLECTED IN ME
AND NOW I EMBRACE SUFFERING,
NOT LOOKING AT THE BEGINNING,
BUT THE END BECAUSE HAVING DONE ALL, I WIN.

SUFFERING IS MY LONG, LOST KIN;
AFFLICTION IS HIS BROTHER,
AND IF YOU LOOK OVER THERE YOU'LL SEE FIERY TRIALS—
YEAH, THAT'S THEIR MOTHER.

NOW'S THE TIME TO RECEIVE MY CROWN
AND I'M PRESENTED TO THE LORD OF MY BEING—
MY GOD, MY EVERYTHING!
NO NEED FOR INTRODUCTION,
HE KNOWS HIS PRODUCTION AND MY NEW NAME.
THE ANGELS SING, "REDEEMED, REDEEMED!"

AND I THANK YOU, SUFFERING,
FOR MAKING ME INTO THE IMAGE OF MY KING!

Reflection 7

IN A WORLD FULL OF SO MUCH CHAOS, IT'S EASY TO LET WORRY AND FEAR HAVE THEIR WAY INSTEAD OF TRUSTING IN GOD. FOR THE MOST PART, FEAR IS OUR FIRST RESPONSE. WE DO NOT AUTOMATICALLY TURN TO THE WORD OF GOD TO FIND OUR PEACE—BUT WE SHOULD. IN HIS WORD IS THE ANSWER FOR EVERYTHING THAT AILS US. WHATEVER WE NEED CAN BE FOUND THERE.

GOD TELLS US TO CAST ALL OUR CARES UPON HIM BECAUSE HE CARES FOR US. HE TELLS US TO BE ANXIOUS FOR NOTHING BUT IN EVERYTHING BY PRAYER AND SUPPLICATION, WITH THANKSGIVING, LET OUR REQUESTS BE MADE KNOWN. WHEN WE DO THAT, WHAT COMES NEXT IS THE PEACE OF GOD, WHICH PASSES ALL UNDERSTANDING. THIS PEACE THEN GUARDS OUR HEARTS AND MINDS! SEE HOW THE WORD WORKS. HE HAS NOT GIVEN US A SPIRIT OF FEAR, SO DON'T LIVE BY IT—IT'S NOT YOURS!

PEACE, BE STILL

PEACE, BE STILL.

WHEN I FIND MYSELF RUNNIN' FROM HIS WILL,
WHEN MY SOUL IS DISQUIETED, SO LOUD AND HARD TO KILL,
I SUFFER DEVASTATION, BUT GETTING BACK UP,
I ASK YOU LORD TO FILL MY CUP 'TIL IT RUNS OVER
AND I'M OVERCOME WITH THE BLESSINGS
THAT MAKETH RICH FOR A WRETCH UNDONE

I'M FREE, BUT AT TIMES I LIVE LIKE I'M BOUND.
OUTSIDE I SMILE, BUT INWARDLY I FROWN.
WHY ARE YOU SO CAST DOWN?
ROAR LIKE A LION, OH DAUGHTER OF ZION.

LET PEACE BE STILL
WHERE THERE WERE SILENT SCREAMS AND INNER TURMOILS,
UNCLEAN, UNCLEAN WITH LEPROSY AND BOILS.
HE BROUGHT MY SIN TO THE SEA OF FORGETFULNESS
AS FAR AS THE EAST IS FROM THE WEST.

HE LED ME BESIDE THE STILL WATER,
VERY PROTECTIVE AS MY FATHER.
THE STORMS ARE RAGING
BUT THIS TIME I'M NOT RUNNING, BUT SEEKING HIS WILL,
I LOOK TO THE HILLS
AND SAY, "PEACE, BE STILL."

Reflection 8

THE DEVIL'S STRATEGY IS TO KILL, STEAL, AND DESTROY, AND HE COMES FOR THOSE WHO DO NOT PLACE THEIR HOPE AND TOTAL TRUST IN THE LORD, LEAVING THEMSELVES OPEN TO ATTACK. ONE OF THE MAIN WAYS WE CAN DEFEAT THE ENEMY IS SURPRISINGLY THROUGH OUR PRAISE. DO YOU SUFFER FROM DEPRESSION? THE WORD OF GOD PRESCRIBES THE GARMENT OF PRAISE.

PRAISE WAS USED TO TEAR DOWN THE WALLS OF JERICHO. IT SHOOK THE EARTH AND OPENED UP PRISON DOORS FOR PAUL AND SILAS! PRAISE SHIFTS THE FOCUS FROM YOU TO GOD. HE WANTS YOU TO CAST THOSE CARES ON HIM BECAUSE HE CARES FOR YOU!

STAY IN THE WORD AND PRAYER. STAY IN THE FIGHT, DON'T CRACK BECAUSE THE DEVIL IS LOOKING FOR THE SLIGHTEST OPENING SO HE CAN BUST THAT WALL OF DEFENSE DOWN. PUT THE WHOLE ARMOR ON DAILY. NO WEAPON FORMED AGAINST YOU WILL PROSPER! THE VICTORY IS WON WHEN YOU PRAISE!

MY WEAPON

YOU THINK I'M DOWN FOR THE COUNT BUT DON'T COUNT ME OUT.
PRAISE IS WHAT I DO TO MAKE IT THROUGH.

IT'S COMELY FOR THE UPRIGHT, NOT THE UPTIGHT.
SO COME OUT OF YOUR SHOES,
YOU'VE GOT NOTHING TO LOSE.

DANCE LIKE DAVID DANCED, NOT WORRYING ABOUT CIRCUMSTANCE.
KEEP PRESSIN' ON PRAISE UNTIL DAWN.
DON'T LET GO 'TIL HE BLESSES YOU; PRAISE IS WHAT YOU DO.

THE ENEMY BECOMES CONFUSED AND DISTRAUGHT,
'CAUSE WITH EVERY TACTIC YOU FOUGHT.
HE'S SHAKIN' HIS CHAINS AND WRACKIN' HIS BRAIN;
OUR WEAPONS HE DISDAINS.

WHAT I SOWED IN TEARS, I'LL REAP IN JOY LIKE A CHILD
EMBRACING THAT FAVORITE CHRISTMAS TOY.
I WENT WALKIN' THROUGH THE VALLEY OF THE SHADOW OF DEATH
AND FEARED NO EVIL.
MY GOD PERFORMED AN UPHEAVAL.
LOOKED AROUND SAW MY BONES QUAKE AND SHAKE,
CAUSING MY EARTH TO MOVE.

THE SPIRIT PUT THEM TOGETHER AND GAVE ME A NEW GROOVE.
I STARTED HUMMIN' AND PROCEEDED TO CLAP AND SHOUT.
THIS TIME, I KNEW I WAS COMIN' OUT.

I SHALL NOT BE MOVED.
LIKE A TREE, YOU'LL KNOW ME BY MY FRUIT.
NOT JUST THE SURFACE, BUT ALL THE WAY DOWN TO THE ROOT.

DON'T STOP NOW; KEEP IT COMIN'!
I'M NO LONGER WALKIN', I'M RUNNIN'.
FOR MY LIFE, GOTTA FIGHT FOR WHAT'S RIGHT.
THAT'S ALL YOU GOT? 'CAUSE I'M NOT TIRED YET,
JUST BREAKIN' OUT IN A LITTLE SWEAT.

GOT SOME REGRETS BUT NOW I SEE IT MADE FOR A BETTER ME,
NOW MY HANDS ARE RAISED,
FOR MY WEAPON IS MY PRAISE

Reflection 9

FORGIVENESS, WHETHER FOR SOMEONE ELSE OR YOURSELF, CAN BE DIFFICULT. WHEN YOU HAVE DONE THINGS YOU KNOW YOU SHOULDN'T HAVE DONE, YOU WILL BEGIN TO HIT THE REPLAY BUTTON AGAIN AND AGAIN, WISHING YOU WOULD HAVE DONE SOME THINGS DIFFERENTLY. IT WON'T CHANGE WHAT HAPPENED, SO THERE IS NO USE BEATING YOURSELF UP ABOUT IT. JUST PICK YOURSELF UP AND TRY AGAIN, RIGHT? EASIER SAID THAN DONE.

AS MENTIONED EARLIER, YOU START TO BEAT YOURSELF UP WITH THE "WHY WOULD I DO THAT, AND WHY DIDN'T I LEAVE THAT SITUATION?" WE HOLD OURSELVES PRISONERS EVEN AFTER GOD HAS FREED AND FORGIVEN US, ACTING LIKE, "GOD, YOUR FORGIVENESS IS NOT ENOUGH! I DON'T DESERVE IT! PUNISH ME! DON'T FORGIVE ME!" WHEN WE DO THAT, WE MAKE OURSELVES GOD! LORD, FORGIVE ME FOR THE MANY TIMES I'VE DONE THAT.

WHEN OTHERS HAVE OFFENDED OR DONE YOU WRONG, FORGIVE THEM. IT MAY NOT BE EASY OR FEEL LIKE IT'S GOING AWAY, BUT WITH THE LORD'S HELP IT WILL HAPPEN. FORGIVE AS YOU WANT TO BE FORGIVEN. IT TAKES COURAGE TO DO THAT BECAUSE YOU HAVE YOUR OWN FEELINGS AND PERSPECTIVE ABOUT THE SITUATION AND SO DOES THE OTHER PERSON. OTHERS MAY THINK YOU'RE CRAZY IF YOU FORGIVE FOR WHAT WE CALL "MAJOR OFFENSES," BUT IN THE END, FORGIVENESS IS FOR YOU. IT RELEASES YOU TO LOVE AND ENJOY LIFE. NOBODY IS SAYING GO BACK TO THE DOG THAT BIT YOU, BUT FORGIVENESS IS FOR YOUR OWN HEALING AND RESTORATION. RELEASE THE PERSON AND FREE YOURSELF.

IF I SAY I FORGIVE

IF I SAY I FORGIVE WHY MUST I CONSTANTLY REMIND?
MAKING TIME REWIND,
BECOMES LIKE POKING OUT THE EYES OF THE BLIND.
IF I SAY I FORGIVE BUT WON'T FORGET, HERE'S WHERE I LACK.
I GIVE YOU A GIFT, BUT WHEN I'M READY, YOU HAVE TO GIVE IT BACK.

DOES THAT MAKE ANY SENSE? NO, THERE HAS TO BE A BALANCE.
WE LOOK IN THE MIRROR AND FORGET OUR REFLECTION.
WHAT WAS THE PURPOSE OF THE DEATH, BURIAL, AND RESURRECTION?
WE CONDEMN YOU FOR NOT BEING THE PICTURE OF PERFECTION.

WHO ARE WE TO SAY, "TODAY YOU LIVE,
BUT TOMORROW YOU'LL SURELY DIE!"?
WE SIT IN THE JUDGMENT SEAT ONLY MEANT FOR THE MOST HIGH.
GOD ALONE DECIDES HOW ONE REAPS WHAT THEY HAVE SOWED.
WE TRY TO FORCE THEM TO CARRY INSTEAD OF BURY THEIR HEAVY LOAD.

IF I SAY I FORGIVE, THEN I NEED TO LET GO
AND LET THE STRONG WIND OF THE SPIRIT BLOW
BLOW INTO ME GOD; DON'T JUST BREATHE
'CAUSE THE FORCE OF YOUR BLOW IS STRONGER THAN YOUR BREEZE.

I NEED THEE, OH I NEED THEE, BECAUSE IT'S ME STANDING IN THE NEED.
GOTTA GET THE BEAM BEFORE ATTEMPTING TO GET OUT THE SPECK.
GOTTA LOOK WITHIN BEFORE NOTICING YOUR SIN.
THIS IS HOW WE BOTH WIN.
FALL TO OUR KNEES AND THEN TRULY KNOW WHAT IT MEANS TO LET GO
AND LIVE IF I SAY I FORGIVE.

Reflection 10

THERE WAS A TIME IN MY LIFE WHEN I CONSTANTLY REPLAYED THE MISTAKES I MADE THROUGHOUT MY LIFE. SOME OF THEM WERE EASY ONES THAT COULD HAVE BEEN AVOIDED WHILE OTHERS I NEEDED TO GO THROUGH WITH A FINE-TOOTHED COMB TO KNOW, *I SHOULDN'T HAVE GONE THAT WAY.* DID IT DO ME ANY GOOD TO REPLAY IT IN MY MIND OR DID IT CHANGE ANYTHING THAT HAPPENED? NO, IT DIDN'T BUT SOMEHOW IT KIND OF MADE ME FEEL BETTER TO GO BACK AND BEAT MYSELF UP FOR THE DUMB DECISIONS I MADE.

IT WAS SO HARD LETTING GO OF THE THINGS I FAILED AT. I DIDN'T REALIZE MY FAILURES WERE LEARNING EXPERIENCES. I WASN'T SUPPOSED TO STOP AT THE FAILURES BUT WAS TO CONTINUE ON TO MY SUCCESS. AN ANONYMOUS WRITER WROTE, "DON'T JUDGE YOUR YEAR ONE BY SOMEONE'S YEAR FIFTY." I CANNOT JUDGE MY YESTERDAY BY WHAT I KNOW TODAY. EACH LEVEL BRINGS MORE EXPERIENCE, KNOWLEDGE, AND THE WISDOM TO KNOW WHEN TO LET GO.

LET GO

I LET GO OF MY PAST, I DON'T KNOW WHEN,
BUT I REALIZED I WASN'T LOOKIN' BACK AGAIN.
WHEN DELIVERANCE COMES AT TIMES YOU ARE UNAWARE
UNTIL INTO THE FACE OF TEMPTATION YOU DO STARE,
THIS TIME STANDING SURE-FOOTED, NO DOUBT,
NOT THINKIN' ABOUT IT, BUT GOD, YOU BROUGHT ME OUT!

I'M AT PEACE WHERE NORMALLY I WOULD RESPOND.
I'M IN MY HIDING PLACE WHERE THE ENEMY CAN DO ME NO HARM.
YEAH THERE'S A THOUSAND MORE I HAVE TO OVERCOME,
BUT THANK GOD,
I PASSED THIS ONE.

GOD GIVE ME WISDOM WHERE I LACK.
HELP ME TO PRESS FORWARD AND NOT LOOK BACK.
IF I DO, I'M NOT FIT FOR THE KINGDOM.
I THANK GOD FOR MY FREEDOM.
HELP MY FELLOW MAN
WHERE I CAN.

NOT THAT I'M BETTER THAN YOU,
BUT IF I MADE IT THROUGH,
WHY NOT YOU, TOO?
I DON'T HAVE ALL THE ANSWERS,
BUT I'VE HAD SOME SPIRITUAL CANCERS.

SO THERE ARE AREAS I CAN HELP YOU AVOID.
DON'T BE DESTROYED
I BEND, BUT DON'T BREAK,
MADE BEAUTIFUL MISTAKES.
FROM EVERY ONE I'VE LEARNED,
NOT RIGHT AWAY, BUT I EVENTUALLY TURNED.

SOMETIMES WEARY,
I START TO LET GO.
IT IS HERE THAT I BEGIN TO GROW.
I'M RIGHT WHERE GOD WANTS ME TO BE,
NO EARTHLY ENERGY
SHOWING ME WHERE THIS BATTLE TRULY BELONGS—
GIVING ME A REASON TO SING MY SONG.

WHEN ENOUGH IS ENOUGH, LORD, HELP ME TO LOOK UP.
GIVE ME THE PEACE THAT PASSES ALL UNDERSTANDING,
OF MYSELF I'M TOO DEMANDING
BUT THERE IS NO CONDEMNATION WITH RESTORATION,
LET THE WORLD SEE YOUR TRANSFORMATION.

GLORIFY YOUR FATHER IN HEAVEN
LORD, IF I STUMBLE DON'T LET ME BE AFRAID TO ASK FOR ASSISTANCE.
PUT ON THE WHOLE ARMOR, HELP ME TO BUILD A RESISTANCE.
TO THE ONE THAT THINKS HE STANDS, TAKE HEED LEST HE FALL.
JESUS, YOU ARE LORD OF ALL.
OF THESE THINGS I BOLDLY PROCLAIM;
LORD, DO IT ALL IN YOUR PRECIOUS NAME

Reflection 11

MANY OF US, ESPECIALLY WOMEN, HAVE A TENDENCY NOT TO BE SATISFIED IN SOME FORM OR ANOTHER WITH OUR OUTWARD APPEARANCE. SOMETIMES WE FEEL TOO DARK, TOO LIGHT, TOO TALL, TOO SHORT, TOO FAT, TOO SKINNY, AND THE LIST GOES ON AND ON. IT CAN BE HARD TO COME TO THE POINT OF APPRECIATION FOR HOW WE ARE FEARFULLY AND WONDERFULLY MADE. WE DO NOT HAVE TO COMPARE OURSELVES TO SOMEONE ELSE, WISHING WE WERE THEM WHEN AT THE SAME TIME THEY ARE PROBABLY WISHING THEY WERE US! EMBRACE THE PERSON GOD HAS CALLED YOU TO BE ALONG WITH THE FEATURES HE GAVE YOU.

WE DON'T NEED A WORLD FULL OF CLONES IN LOOKS AND BEHAVIORS. WHO SET THE STANDARD OF BEAUTY? IT VARIES FROM ONE OPINION TO ANOTHER. IT IS IN THE EYE OF THE BEHOLDER. EVERYBODY PLAYS A PART IN THIS THING CALLED LIFE AND IF YOU WASTE IT TRYING TO BE OR COMPARE YOURSELF TO SOMEONE ELSE, YOU MISS OUT ON THE AUTHENTIC YOU. NO MATTER WHO YOU LOOK LIKE IN YOUR FAMILY THERE IS ONLY ONE UNIQUELY- MADE YOU AND THE WORLD WOULDN'T BE THE SAME WITHOUT YOU IN IT.

FEARFULLY AND WONDERFULLY MADE

YOU KNEW ME BEFORE I WAS FORMED
IN MY MOTHER'S WOMB, BORN AND SHAPED IN SIN AND INIQUITY.
YOU KNEW ME.
THE VERY HAIRS OF MY HEAD ARE NUMBERED,
BEFORE YOU I AM UNCOVERED.

NOTHING HIDDEN, MY LIFE EXPOSED—
NO LONGER FULLY CLOTHED.
IN THE HANDS OF THE POTTER, I AM PLIABLE.
HIS LOVE FOR ME IS SO UNDENIABLE—
A LOVE I CAN'T EXPLAIN.

I'VE BEEN CAPTURED AND CHANGED;
HE'S MADE ME A LITTLE LOWER THAN THE ANGELS
AND YES, I'M BRANDED—
LIKE SHEEP, I WALK WHERE I'M COMMANDED.

NOT MY OWN, BUT BOUGHT WITH A PRICE,
SEEN AS A PRECIOUS PEARL—
GOD'S LITTLE GIRL.
REDEEMED AND SEALED BY CHRIST WITH THE GIFT OF EVERLASTING LIFE.

WHO AM I?
I AM HIS AND HE IS MINE,
FROM NOW UNTIL THE END OF TIME.

Reflection 12

Jesus posed the question to His disciples, "Who do men say I am?" They answered according to what they heard. Then Jesus asked the same question, but in a more intimate way, "Who do *you* say I am?" This would hit home because these men walked with Jesus so they were close to Him and would know better than anybody else. I could just imagine what was going on when Jesus asked that question. All the disciples were probably sitting there thinking, "I'm not answering that question, you answer it!"

Peter was the only one bold enough to answer that question personally, saying, "Thou art the Christ, the Son of the living God!" I'm sure he had a moment of pride when he found out he had given the correct answer. That moment would be short-lived, however, because as we know, Peter would later deny even being a follower of the man he had just perfectly described. Who is He? God Almighty, the Prince of Peace.

WHO IS HE?

WHO IS WORTHY TO BREAK THE SEALS AND OPEN THE SCROLL?
OH, HOW I WEPT AND WEPT
NO ONE WAS FOUND WORTHY TO DO ANYTHING
THEN ONE OF THE ELDERS SAID:

"DON'T WEEP.
SEE THE LION OF THE TRIBE OF JUDAH,
THE ROOT OF DAVID HAS TRIUMPHED.
HE IS ABLE TO OPEN THE SCROLL AND ITS SEVEN SEALS."

THEN I SAW A LAMB LOOKING AS IF
IT HAD BEEN SLAIN AT THE CENTER OF THE THRONE
AND WHEN HE TOOK THE SCROLL LIVING CREATURES
AND ELDERS FELL DOWN BEFORE HIM.

THEY HAD HARPS AND OUR PRAYERS.
THEN I HEARD THE VOICE OF TEN THOUSAND TIMES
TEN THOUSAND ANGELS SAYING LOUDLY,
"WORTHY IS THE LAMB WHO WAS SLAIN TO RECEIVE POWER, WEALTH,
WISDOM, STRENGTH, HONOR, GLORY AND PRAISE!" (REVELATION 5).

MY DEAREST LORD,
YOU CAME ON THIS EARTH, BORN TO DIE,
NOT BECAUSE OF YOUR OWN SIN, BUT MINE.

WHEN I HEARD THE NEWS, MY HEART WAS BROKEN,
NOT A WORD WAS SPOKEN.
THE ALMIGHTY TURNED HIS HEAD AS YOU BLED.
YOU FELT FORSAKEN AS THE EARTH WAS SHAKEN,
YOU WERE THE ONLY OPTION.
LIFE ETERNAL THROUGH ADOPTION.

YOU CHOSE TO COME DOWN
MERCY WAS FOUND,
WEARING THORNS FOR A CROWN,
DEATH-WITH LIFTED ARMS THOUGHT HE HAD YOU BOUND.

THREE DAYS LATER THE CREATOR
TOOK DEATH BY THE THROAT,
LEFT A RETURN-TO-SENDER NOTE.
ROSE WITH ALL POWER IN HIS HAND,
THE GRAVE COULDN'T WITHSTAND
THE ULTIMATE SACRIFICE,
THE ONE TO SAVE MY LIFE.

ALL HAIL TO THE KING WHO CAUSES DEMONS TO FLEE
AT THE MENTION OF HIS NAME.
THE TIDES HAVE SHIFTED.
BLINK AND YOU'LL MISS IT.
IN A MOMENT, IN THE TWINKLING OF AN EYE,
AS SURE AS THE NAILS WERE DRIVEN,
HE IS RISEN!

Reflection 13

SOMETIMES YOU WILL FIND YOURSELF CONFUSED ABOUT SO MANY THINGS, YOUR EMOTIONS CARRYING YOU EVERYWHERE! I WILL SAY THAT IT IS IMPORTANT TO WATCH THE PEOPLE YOU SURROUND YOURSELF WITH BECAUSE THEY WILL PLAY A MAJOR PART IN HOW YOU VIEW THINGS. IF YOU SURROUND YOURSELF WITH "DEBBIE DOWNERS," YOU WILL SOON FIND YOURSELF RAINING ON EVERYONE'S PARADE, INCLUDING YOUR OWN. IF YOU SURROUND YOURSELF WITH POSITIVE PEOPLE, YOU'LL FIND YOURSELF BEING OPTIMISTIC, SEEKING THE LIGHT AT THE END OF EVERY TUNNEL.

THE BIBLE GIVES US CLEAR EXAMPLES OF HOW WE SHOULD THINK; WHETHER OR NOT WE FOLLOW THROUGH IS UP TO US. WHEN YOU FIND YOURSELF CONFUSED AND NOT KNOWING WHICH WAY TO TURN, THAT'S THE TIME TO PRAY AND SEEK GOD'S FACE FOR ANSWERS. HE IS NOT THE AUTHOR OF CONFUSION. HE WILL LEAD AND GUIDE YOU INTO ALL TRUTH, JUST ASK HIM.

SOMETIMES I . . .

SOMETIMES I WONDER WHY I HAVE TO BE THE ONE
TO LAY DOWN AND DIE,
WHEN ALL I WANT TO DO IS CRY AND
SAY GOODBYE TO THE THINGS THAT HAVE BECOME
A THORN IN MY SIDE.
BUT EVERY DAY I STOP AND SAY HELLO
TO THE FRIENDS I'VE COME TO KNOW
LIKE MRS. WHY ME AND MR. HOW COULD THIS BE
AND THE INFAMOUS OH GOD, CAN'T YOU SEE?

I DO WELL TO PRAISE, BUT THIS IS ONE OF THEM DAYS
I WANNA SCREAM, MAKE A SCENE—
YOU KNOW WHAT I MEAN?

FIRST RESPONSE NOT ALWAYS RIGHT, THOUGH I TRY WITH ALL MY MIGHT,
BUT SOMETIMES I . . .

FEEL LIKE I . . .
LOOK LIKE I . . .
ACT LIKE I . . .
WALK LIKE I . . .
TALK LIKE I . . .
GOD ONLY KNOWS WHY I . . .

YOU FILL IN THE BLANKS, 'CAUSE SOMETIMES I . . .

DE ANDREA DUDLEY

Reflection 14

THERE'S SO MUCH WAR GOING ON IN THE LAND. I'M NOT TALKING ABOUT THE ARMED FORCES, BUT WAR ON THE STREETS. COPS ARE KILLING PEOPLE OF COLOR, MOSTLY WITHOUT A CAUSE AND THE MAJORITY ARE MEN. ALWAYS AFRAID TO TURN ON THE NEWS FOR FEAR OF SEEING ONE MORE BLACK MAN KILLED BY POLICE JUSTIFYING THEIR MEANS TO AN END ALONG WITH A JUSTICE SYSTEM THAT HAS BEEN ANYTHING BUT. THOSE WHOM WE COUNT ON TO PROTECT AND SERVE HAVE NOW BECOME THE ONES WE FEAR THE MOST OR VICE VERSA. THIS RELATIONSHIP STRAIN IS SEEMINGLY BEYOND REPAIR. NEXT YOU HAVE THE BLACK-ON-BLACK CRIME, WHICH MAKES NO SENSE AT ALL. WE DON'T EVEN NEED THE POLICE TO KILL US; WE'RE DOING JUST FINE BY OURSELVES. ONE DISAGREEMENT, WRONG LOOK, OR "DISRESPECT" FROM ONE TO ANOTHER AND BOOM—A CHERISHED LIFE IS SNUFFED OUT, LEAVING FAMILIES TO GRIEVE. GONE ARE THE DAYS WHERE PEOPLE FOUGHT AND LIVED TO TELL THEIR STORY. WHAT'S GOING ON?

WHAT'S GOIN' ON?

IS IT BLUE-ON-BLACK OR IS IT BLACK-ON-BLACK?
TRUTH IS, IT GOES WAY DEEPER THAN THAT.

OUR FIGHT IS NOT AGAINST FLESH AND BLOOD,
BUT THE ENEMY HAD US THINKING IT WAS.

THE REAL BATTLE IS AGAINST THE THINGS WE CAN'T SEE,
THE THINGS THAT MAKE US HIT OUR KNEES—
LIKE PRINCIPALITIES, POWERS, RULERS OF THE DARKNESS OF THIS WORLD
AND SPIRITUAL WICKEDNESS IN HIGH PLACES.

YES, WE NEED TO LAY ON OUR FACES,
GET EQUIPPED, DON'T QUIT,
TAKE DOMINION AND NOT OPINIONS.

GET IN POSITION, MAKE THE DECISION AND
CRY OUT TO THE GOD OF OUR SALVATION.

NO NEED FOR RESERVATION,
COME BOLD BEFORE THE THRONE AND
MAKE THE SECRET PLACE YOUR HOME.

STAY ON TRACK, NO TIME FOR SLACK
YOU PUT YOUR HAND TO THE PLOW,
DON'T YOU DARE LOOK BACK NOW.

TAKE NO PRISONERS FOR WE ARE WINNERS,
THE WEAPONS MAY FORM BUT WILL NEVER PROSPER
AGAINST THOSE WHO CARRY THE GOSPEL.

Reflection 15

AS PARENTS, WE WANT SO MUCH FOR OUR CHILDREN. FROM THE TIME WE FIRST HOLD THEM UNTIL THEY ARE OFF ON THEIR OWN, WE WISH THEM NOTHING BUT THE BEST THAT LIFE HAS TO OFFER. WE DESIRE THEM TO BE CONTRIBUTORS AND NOT MENACES TO SOCIETY. THE WORLD IS THEIR OYSTER. THE PICTURE WE PAINT FOR OUR CHILDREN, HOWEVER, DOESN'T ALWAYS WORK OUT THAT WAY BECAUSE THERE ARE BUMPS AND ROADBLOCKS ALONG THE WAY. OUR JOB AS PARENTS IS TO BE THAT ENCOURAGING VOICE OF REASON, THAT SHOULDER TO LEAN ON, AND THE ONE WHO WILL ALWAYS KEEP THEM LIFTED UP IN PRAYER NO MATTER WHAT IT LOOKS LIKE. DON'T LET PRAYER BE THE ONLY THING YOU CAN DO FOR YOUR CHILDREN; LET IT BE THE BEST THING.

A MOTHER'S PRAYER

FATHER GOD, IN THE MIGHTY NAME OF JESUS,
I GIVE BACK TO YOU WHAT YOU HAVE GIVEN TO ME
AND PLACE THEM IN YOUR HAND.
FOR IT'S ONLY BY YOUR GRACE AND MERCY
THAT EACH OF MY SONS WILL LIVE TO BE A MAN.

I THANK YOU THAT NONE WILL BE LOST
BECAUSE YOU PAID THE COST.
FORGIVE ME FOR THE TIMES I FAILED
AND DIDN'T KNOW WHAT TO DO
WHILE GOING THROUGH—
I WAS SUCH A WRECK.

SO MANY TIMES, YOU HAD TO PUT ME IN CHECK.
LORD, BE MY INSTRUCTION MANUAL,
FOR WITH ONE
THEY DID NOT COME.

LEAD AND GUIDE ME INTO ALL TRUTH
'CAUSE SATAN'S ON THE LOOSE
DEVOURING THOSE NOT ON GUARD,
FACES MARRED.

LORD HELP ME TO LOOK TO THE HILLS AND KNOW
THE SEEDS THAT HAVE FALLEN ON ALL TYPES OF GROUND WILL GROW
FOR THEY HAVE BEEN ENTRUSTED TO YOU.

THE GOOD AND THE BAD
WITH WHAT LITTLE FAITH I HAD.
YOU SAID, ALL I NEED
WAS THE GRAIN OF A MUSTARD SEED.

YOU SAID, I COULD SPEAK A THING AND IT COULD BE SO,
WHICH LETS ME KNOW MY WORDS WERE CREATED TO SPEAK LIFE, NOT STRIFE.
THERE IS POWER IN MY TONGUE,
SO TODAY I SPEAK LIFE INTO THE FRUIT OF MY WOMB,
OF MY LABOR, MY SONS.
YOU ARE WISE AS SERPENTS, HARMLESS AS DOVES.

YOU ARE NOT BENEATH, BUT ABOVE;
YOU ARE THE HEAD AND NOT THE TAIL—
EVEN WHEN YOU FAIL, YOU STILL PREVAIL.
BE WHO GOD HAS ORDAINED YOU TO BE
NOT THE STEREOTYPICAL BLACK MAN RUNNING THE STREETS.
YOU ARE FUTURE KINGS AND MORE THAN CONQUERORS
MY SONS, RISE UP BECAUSE YOU ARE WARRIORS!

Reflection 16

BEING A CHRISTIAN WITHOUT THE WORD IS LIKE GOING TO WORK UNDRESSED. YOU WOULDN'T GO TO WAR WITHOUT YOUR WEAPONS OR LEAVE YOUR HOME OR CAR IN THE HANDS OF A ROBBER, WOULD YOU? THAT'S WHAT HAPPENS WHEN WE GO THROUGH LIFE AS CHILDREN OF GOD WITHOUT OPENING THE BIBLE OR TAKING TIME TO BE IN HIS PRESENCE. YOU WANT THE FINISHED WORK WITHOUT THE LABOR. YOU WANT THE BEAUTY WITHOUT FACING THE BEAST. IT DOESN'T HAPPEN THAT WAY.

THERE'S AN OLD PHRASE, "NO GUTS, NO GLORY!" THAT SAYING STILL HOLDS TRUE. YOU CAN'T GET WHAT YOU WANT WITHOUT DOING WHAT YOU NEED TO DO TO GET IT. YOU CANNOT HALF STEP. A GATE WITH NO FENCE AROUND IT IS USELESS! YOU HAVE TO BE WILLING TO DO WHAT NEEDS TO BE DONE TO GUARD THE PRECIOUS JEWEL CALLED YOUR SOUL. DON'T LEAVE IT UNPROTECTED.

I GOT A GATE

I GOT A GATE WITH NO FENCE AROUND IT,
WHICH LEAVES ME UNPROTECTED AND DEFECTIVE.
I CARRY THE WORD,
BUT GOD'S VOICE I HAVEN'T HEARD.

WHY? 'CAUSE I CHOOSE NOT TO OPEN
AND READ WHAT GOD HAS SPOKEN
COME TO CHURCH WITH NO INTENTION OF GETTIN' RIGHT.
GOD WANTS TO SAVE MY LIFE,
BUT I PUT UP A FIGHT.

WHO SAID TOMORROW IS PROMISED TO ME?
YET I'M LIVING LIKE I KNOW IT TO BE.
EVEN WITH MY THOUGHTS, I THINK THINGS I OUGHT NOT.
I GOT A GATE, BUT MY SIN'S SO PLEASIN'
THAT MAKES MY GATE, A GATE FOR NO REASON.

LORD, I'M CALLING ON YOU, AND AT THE SAME TIME,
FOLLOWING MY ADDICTION
WHICH CREATES FRICTION.
LORD, BE A FENCE ALL AROUND ME, THIS I PRAY,
WHILE LOOKING FOR A WAY OUT.

DON'T TAKE OFFENSE, BUT THIS JUST MAKES NO SENSE.
IT WAS A PART OF MY LIFE,
WHICH MAKES IT SO EASY TO WRITE.
WHILE TEARS WERE RUNNING DOWN MY EYES, I CRIED
"LORD, PLEASE DON'T CRACK THE SKY.
I'M IN BETWEEN THESE SHEETS
MY FLESH IS SO WEAK."

ALL THAT MAN DID WAS SMILE;
NEXT THING YOU KNOW I'M HAVING HIS CHILD
I GOT A GATE, BUT MY SIN'S SO PLEASIN'
THAT MAKES MY GATE, THE GATE FOR NO REASON.

MY PEOPLE, THINK BEFORE YOU DO,
'CAUSE THE NEXT ONE YOU HURT MAY GO BEYOND YOU.
DON'T BLAME GOD WHEN YOUR LIFE BECOMES MORE THAN HARD
TAKE A LOOK WITHIN AND SEE THE DESTRUCTION
THAT CAME FROM LEAVIN' YOUR GATE WIDE OPEN
WITH A FENCE THAT'S BROKEN
I GOT A GATE, BUT MY SIN'S SO PLEASIN',
THAT MAKES MY GATE, THE GATE FOR NO REASON.

Reflection 17

WHEN A MAN AND A WOMAN REACH THE POINT OF MATRIMONY IN THEIR RELATIONSHIP, PLEASE KNOW THAT THIS IS THE MOST SOLEMN COVENANT YOU CAN MAKE ON EARTH. AFTER THE WEDDING'S SPARKLE AND SHINE ARE GONE, IT'S THEN TIME FOR THE MARRIAGE JOURNEY. THIS UNION IS TO REFLECT CHRIST'S RELATIONSHIP TO THE CHURCH, HIS BODY. HOW YOU TREAT YOUR HUSBAND OR WIFE IS HOW YOU RELATE TO GOD. YOUR SPOUSE IS NOT JUST YOUR SPOUSE, BUT A SOUL, A CHILD OF GOD, SO IT'S NOT ACCEPTABLE FOR YOU TO TREAT THEM IN WHATEVER MANNER YOU PLEASE BECAUSE YOU BOTH NOW CARRY THE SAME LAST NAME.

IN THIS JOURNEY, ALL THE THINGS THAT USED TO BE SO CUTE AND TOLERABLE FOR YOU CAN BECOME A NUISANCE AND MAKES YOUR SKIN CRAWL. YOU HAVE TO CONDITION YOURSELF DAILY TO LEARN ABOUT AND FIGURE OUT SOMEBODY ELSE. IT'S NOT JUST ABOUT YOU ANYMORE. YOU CAN'T COME AND GO AS YOU PLEASE. THIS IS NOW A TIME OF ACCOUNTABILITY TO SOMEONE ELSE THAT'S NOT YOUR PARENT. THIS PERSON'S UPBRINGING MAY NOT HAVE BEEN THE SAME AS YOURS. WHAT MAY BE SECOND NATURE IN YOUR EYES, MAY TAKE SOME EFFORT FOR YOUR MATE.

YOU HAVE TO LEAVE AND CLEAVE IN ORDER TO CULTIVATE AND NURTURE WHAT THE LORD HAS JOINED TOGETHER. THIS CAN BE VERY HARD FOR EVERYONE INVOLVED, BUT WITH GOD, THIS THREE-FOLD CORD WILL NOT BE EASILY BROKEN.

WHEN TWO BECOME ONE

NOW THE DAY HAS FINALLY COME
WHEN YOU AND I WILL BE AS ONE.
ME, WILL BE REPLACED WITH WE,
AND I WILL FREELY SURRENDER MY POWER
TO MY STRONG TOWER.

YOU PUT THE SPARKLE IN MY EYES, THE DANCE IN MY FEET.
WHAT WAS ONCE PARTIAL IS NOW COMPLETE.
DON'T GET ME WRONG,
I KNOW IT WON'T ALWAYS BE A LOVE SONG.
SOMETIMES WE GOTTA SING THE BLUES,
BUT WE CAN'T LOSE
WHEN IT'S GOD WE CHOOSE.
NEVER WISH TO BE IN ANYONE ELSE'S SHOES.

DON'T BE TOO QUICK;
GO BRICK BY BRICK
BUILD A FIRM FOUNDATION
EVEN THE ALMIGHTY TOOK HIS TIME WITH CREATION.
A WISE WOMAN BUILDS HER HOUSE,
BUT THE FOOLISH ONE TEARS IT DOWN WITH HER OWN HANDS
WOMAN, RESPECT YOUR MAN AND MAN, LOVE YOUR WIFE.
MAY THERE BE NO ENVYING; MAY THERE BE NO STRIFE.
DO EACH OTHER GOOD AND NOT EVIL ALL THE DAYS OF YOUR LIFE.

YOUR PRINCE HAS NOW BECOME YOUR KING
BY PLACING ON YOUR FINGER A WEDDING RING.
'TIL DEATH DO YOU PART
WITH EVERY BEAT OF YOUR HEART,
SPEAK TO EACH OTHER'S SOUL—LET YOUR WORDS BE LIKE GOLD.

BE FRUITFUL AND MULTIPLY.
DON'T LET A DAY GO BY WITHOUT DECLARING YOUR LOVE,
NOT JUST PHILEO, BUT AGAPE FROM ABOVE.
WHO IS LIKE UNTO YOU THE ONE THAT ONLY GOD PRECEDES,
TAKE EACH OTHER TO YOUR DESTINY AND
BRING EACH OTHER TO YOUR KNEES.

DON'T LET THE SUN GO DOWN UPON YOUR WRATH.
IF YOU ACKNOWLEDGE HIM IN ALL YOUR WAYS,
HE'LL DIRECT YOUR PATH
WHEN THE TEARS FLOW JUST KNOW,
THEY ONLY HELP YOU TO GROW.
THE ANGELS REJOICE FOR JOY HAS COME
BECAUSE TWO WILL NOW BECOME ONE.

Reflection 18

IN MARRIAGE, THINGS DON'T ALWAYS END HAPPILY EVER AFTER. SOMETIMES WE ARE HATEFUL AND DETESTABLE, EVEN SOMETIMES ENDING IN DIVORCE. MANY OF US WALK INTO RELATIONSHIPS WITH UNREALISTIC EXPECTATIONS. I KNOW I DID.

WE (I) THINK, "YES, I'M GETTING MARRIED AND LIFE WILL BE THE BEST! I DON'T HAVE TO WORRY ABOUT FORNICATING OR FEELING ALONE. I GET TO DO THINGS WITH OTHER MARRIED COUPLES. I'M TIRED OF HUGGING MY PILLOW, WISHING IT WAS THAT HUSBAND/WIFE I SO LONG FOR."

BUT WHAT IF ONCE YOU GOT MARRIED, YOU STILL FELT SINGLE? WHAT THEN? WHAT WOULD YOU DO? WOULD YOU STAY? EVERYTHING DOESN'T ALWAYS GO AS YOU IMAGINE. SOMETIMES THE ACTUAL WEDDING DAY ENDS UP BEING THE CLOSEST THING TO YOUR DEFINITION OF TRUE LOVE.

WHAT IS LOVE? MOST OF US DON'T KNOW UNTIL WE'RE ACTUALLY IN IT GOING OVER BUMPS AND AROUND CURVES. WE LIVE AND WE LEARN. ONE OF THE PHRASES THAT DEFINES LOVE IS LONG SUFFERING. THAT'S WHEN YOU CAN TRULY SAY YOU LOVE SOMEONE BECAUSE YOU HAVE SUFFERED LONG WITH THEM. YES, THERE ARE MOMENTS OF BIRDS CHIRPING WHILE THE SUN RISES, WITH HEARTS FILLED WITH ROMANTIC LOVE, BUT MANY TIMES IT'S RAIN AND THUNDERSTORMS! HOW DO YOU GET THROUGH IT? WELL, PICK UP YOUR UMBRELLA (THE WORD OF GOD) AND PRAISE YOUR WAY THROUGH IT. SEEK HIS WISDOM ABOUT WHAT YOU SHOULD DO. THE QUESTION IS WHEN THINGS AREN'T GOING YOUR WAY, *WHAT IF GOD SAYS STAY?*

WOULD YOU STAY?

WHAT IF GOD TOLD YOU THIS MARRIAGE
WAS TO MAKE YOU HOLY AND NOT HAPPY?
WOULD YOU STAY?

WHAT IF GOD TOLD YOU THAT LIKE HOSEA
YOUR UNION WAS TO EXPRESS "THUS SAITH THE LORD?"
WOULD YOU STAY?

WHAT IF YOUR INVESTMENT SHOWED LITTLE TO NO RETURN?
WOULD YOU STAY?

WHAT IF I TOLD YOU EVERYTHING YOU'VE BEEN THROUGH
IS FOR GOD'S GLORY TO BE REVEALED?
WOULD YOU STAY?

WHAT IF WHAT YOU'RE GOING THROUGH IS
FOR THE SALVATION OF ANOTHER
AND GOD SAYS YOU CAN'T LEAVE; IF YOU DO, THEY WILL DIE?
WOULD YOU STAY?

WHAT IF THE LOVE YOU YEARNED FOR WAS SCATTERED ABROAD?
WOULD YOU STAY?

THERE ARE THINGS GOD REQUIRES OF US
THAT WILL NOT BRING HAPPINESS BUT JOY
BECAUSE WE KNOW WE ARE DOING
WHAT GOD SAYS FOR US TO DO AND HE WANTS US TO OBEY.

THE QUESTION IS, "WOULD YOU STAY?"

Reflection 19

WHEN YOU GO THROUGH LIFE SOMETIMES YOU ARE IN NEED OF RENOVATIONS. THERE ARE TIMES WHEN YOU MAY EVEN NEED A COMPLETE DEMOLITION. EITHER WAY, IF YOU LIVE LONG ENOUGH, THE FEELING OF SPIRITUAL BRICKS BEING KNOCKED OUT OF YOUR WALL WILL COME. YOU WILL FEEL THE BLOW.

WALLS THAT WERE ONCE A FORTIFIED CITY WHERE THE ENEMY HAD NO WAY NOW WIDE OPEN FOR ATTACK. IN HINDSIGHT, YOU CAN SEE WHERE YOU WENT WRONG AND NOW GOD HAS TO PICK UP THE BROKEN PIECES. DON'T FEAR, HE ALWAYS HAS A PLAN. WHEN HE IS DONE, YOU MAY NOT EVEN BE ABLE TO RECOGNIZE YOURSELF BECAUSE YOU WILL LOOK MORE AND MORE LIKE YOUR FATHER. HIS DNA IS BEGINNING TO SHINE THROUGH IN WAYS YOU NEVER THOUGHT POSSIBLE.

NOW EVERY MOVE YOU MAKE AND EVERY BREATH YOU TAKE ARE ORCHESTRATED BY GOD BECAUSE YOU SEE WHERE THE PATH LEADS THAT YOU USUALLY TOOK. HE KNOWS YOU BETTER THAN YOU EVER WILL. TRUST ME, THE FATHER KNOWS BEST AND YOU WANT TO REFLECT HIM. THAT'S WHERE YOUR TRUE IDENTITY CAN BE FOUND. ONLY HE CAN CREATE AND SUSTAIN A NEW AND IMPROVED YOU.

EXTREME MAKEOVER

I WAS A MURDERER, I KILLED WITH MY WORDS.
I SAID A LOT OF PRAYERS NEVER TO BE HEARD

DUE TO THE SIN IN MY LIFE.
IT WAS HARD TO REPRESENT CHRIST.

MY INSIDES WERE DIRTY
AND TRULY UNWORTHY
I HID IT SO WELL,
NO ONE COULD EVER TELL.

THE PERSONAL STRUGGLES I WAS GOING THROUGH,
A TRANSFORMATION BY THE RENEWING OF THE MIND
HAD TO TRULY TAKE IT BY FORCE,
GIVIN' MY OLD SELF AND WAYS A DIVORCE.

OF COURSE, I DIDN'T WILLINGLY SURRENDER MY FLESH DID HINDER,
BUT THE INNER BEAUTY WAS SOMETHING I DID WANT
BECAUSE THE OUTER BECOMES GAUNT.

I AM A CHOSEN GENERATION AND A ROYAL PRIESTHOOD,
BUT IF I DON'T BELIEVE IT WON'T DO ANY GOOD.

LIVING LIKE A PAUPER WHEN I AM A QUEEN,
THE MASTERPIECE THAT REMAINS TO BE SEEN.

WHAT LOOKS FINISHED IS NOT OVER,
I TRUST IN THE POWER OF GOD TO FINISH MY EXTREME MAKEOVER.

Reflection 20

THERE ARE SOME SINS THAT WE CONTINUE TO RETURN TO REGARDLESS OF OUR WILL AND DETERMINATION TO STAY AWAY. YOU WILL STRUGGLE WITH THE SAME THINGS AGAIN AND AGAIN, GOING AROUND THE MULBERRY BUSH UNTIL YOU DECIDE TO TURN IT OVER TO GOD. THIS IS SOMETHING CALLED A *SOUL TIE*—CONNECTING YOUR INNERMOST BEING WITH THAT OF ANOTHER, NOT INTENTIONALLY MEANING TO DO SO. THERE ARE ONES THAT ARE HARMFUL TO YOU, WHETHER PHYSICALLY OR EMOTIONALLY, AND YOU FIND IT HARD TO LET GO. YOU MIGHT FAIL THE FIRST, SECOND, AND THOUSANDTH TIME AROUND, BUT ONE DAY YOU'LL FIND YOURSELF STANDING TALL AGAINST THAT TRIAL OR TEST, MOVING ON, AND NOT LOOKING BACK. THIS WILL NOT BE BY YOUR MIGHT OR POWER, BUT BY GOD'S SPIRIT. THEN YOU WILL BE ABLE TO SAY NO TO THAT OLD FAMILIAR FRIEND.

THAT OLD FAMILIAR FRIEND

THROUGH LIFE CIRCUMSTANCES,
I BECAME FRIENDS WITH BITTERNESS AND STRESS.
WE WERE TWO PEAS IN A POD,
NOBODY COULD SEPARATE US—
NOT EVEN GOD.

HE OFFERED ME FREEDOM, FOR WHICH I TRULY YEARNED
BUT DEDICATION TO MY OLD FAMILIAR FRIENDS CAUSED ME TO RETURN.

THEY SAID THINGS LIKE, "YOU DON'T NEED JOY AND PEACE.
WITH US YOU'RE MORE COMFORTABLE."
BECAUSE YOU KNOW WHAT TO EXPECT.
THERE ARE NO REGRETS."

FREEDOM WILL BRING YOU INTO GOD'S KINGDOM,
BUT THIS IS A PLACE SO STRANGE—
WAITING FOR GOD TO REARRANGE
MY THOUGHTS.

STOP WAITIN' FOR THAT BALL TO DROP;
CATCH IT BEFORE IT HITS THE GROUND.
GOD WILL TURN THINGS AROUND.
TAKE THESE SHACKLES OFF MY FEET,
NO REWIND OR REPEAT.

LEAVE WHAT YOU HAVE CALLED BY THE WRONG NAME,
WHICH CAUSED CONTINUAL PAIN—
THAT WHICH YOU NURTURED AND ALLOWED TO GROW.

EXCUSE AFTER EXCUSE OF THE CONTINUED ABUSE
THAT SO-CALLED LOVER
THAT WE TEND TO COVER.

LET IT GO; RELEASE ITS HAND
AND BECOME AVAILABLE TO GOD'S PLAN.

MY OLD FRIENDS STOPPED BY TODAY TO SAY HELLO
WITH THE SAME OLD PLOT
THIS TIME I RESPONDED WITH "DEPART FROM ME.
I KNOW YOU NOT!"

Reflection 21

YOU KNOW YOU'VE GROWN AS A PERSON WHEN YOU CAN STOP BLAMING EVERYONE ELSE FOR YOUR CURRENT PROBLEMS, LOOK IN THE MIRROR, AND SAY, "IT'S ME, IT'S ME, IT'S ME, OH LORD, STANDING IN THE NEED OF PRAYER!" YES, THAT PERSON OR SITUATION MAY HAVE CONTRIBUTED IN SOME WAYS TO YOUR HARDSHIPS, BUT WHAT'S YOUR RESPONSE? HAVE YOU TAKEN ACCOUNTABILITY FOR HOW YOU WERE RESPONDING? SOMEONE WROTE, "DON'T GET MAD AT THE CLOWN FOR BEING A CLOWN. ASK YOURSELF WHY YOU KEEP GOING TO THE CIRCUS?" THAT HIT HOME FOR ME. I STILL ATTEND THE CIRCUS EVERY NOW AND THEN, BUT ONE DAY, I'M GOING TO RIP UP THE TICKET AND STAY HOME.

I GOT A SECRET

I GOT A SECRET THAT I JUST CAN'T KEEP TO MYSELF.
MY SOUL SAYS "SHHH" BUT MY SPIRIT WANTS TO TELL SOMEBODY ELSE.
NOW THE LORD'S BEEN GOOD TO ME.
HE OPENED MY EYES TO SEE
WHAT I GOTTA DO TO BE FREE.

LISTEN, THIS AIN'T NO BIG REVELATION
TO THE GENERATIONS ACROSS THE NATIONS,
JUST SOMETHING OLD MADE TO LOOK NEW
FOR ME AND FOR YOU.

HOW LONG HAVE WE BEEN SINGING THE BLUES?
"LORD, YOU SEE MY HUSBAND, MY CHILDREN, MY FAMILY, TOO."
THEN I REALIZED THAT INSTEAD OF CONCENTRATING
ON THE MOTE IN MY BROTHER'S EYE,
I NEEDED TO FOCUS ON THE BEAM THAT STUCK OUT OF MINE—
HIGH ENOUGH TO REACH THE SKY.

NOW YOU WOULDN'T BELIEVE THE STUFF COMIN' UP OUT OF MRS. DO GOOD,
LOVE EVERYBODY, GOD'S PERSONAL GIFT TO HER HUSBAND, LITTLE OLE' ME.
THIS WAS MORE THAN I COULD BEAR.
THE LORD TOLD ME NOT TO DESPAIR
FOR HE WAS AWARE

RIGHT NOW, HE'S SHOWING ME HOW TO DEAL WITH ME
FORGET ABOUT WHAT I SEE,
AND WHO DID ME WRONG.
NO MORE OF THAT SAD SONG!

LET GOD BE IN CONTROL.
GET ALL THAT POISON OUT OF YOUR SOUL.
NOW THAT'S MY SECRET;
I TOLD YOU I COULDN'T KEEP IT.

Reflection 22

THIS NEXT POEM IS ENTITLED "UNAWARE" BECAUSE THAT'S EXACTLY WHAT I WAS WHEN I WROTE IT. IT WAS ORIGINALLY A FACEBOOK POST WHERE I QUESTIONED MYSELF ABOUT WHY I WAS HIDING—HIDING FROM WHO I WAS, WHAT I FELT I WANTED TO BE, WHAT I HAVE TO CONTRIBUTE TO THE WORLD, WHO GOD SAYS I TRULY AM, AND WHAT I SHOULD DO ABOUT IT. LEARNING TO BE IMPERFECTLY ME HAS BEEN QUITE A STRUGGLE, BUT BY THE TIME I COMPLETED THE POST, I WAS AMAZED BY HOW BEAUTIFULLY POETIC IT WAS. NOW I WANT TO SHARE IT WITH YOU.

UNAWARE

WHAT DO YOU DO WHEN GOD BURSTS YOUR BUBBLE?
NOT THE KIND OF BUBBLE
WHERE I THINK OF MYSELF MORE HIGHLY THAN I OUGHT,
BUT A BUBBLE WHERE I HIDE,
PROTECTING MYSELF FROM WHAT PEOPLE MAY THINK.

FEAR OF CONFRONTATION—AFRAID TO BE THE AUTHENTIC ME
BECAUSE THERE'S NO WAY SHE CAN REALLY BE LIKE THIS.
AFRAID TO SHARE MY GOD-GIVEN KNOWLEDGE
ALMOST BECOMING A MUTE.

DON'T WANT PEOPLE TO THINK OF ME A CERTAIN WAY.
I CAN'T CONTROL WHAT OTHERS THINK, SAY, OR DO
BUT TELL ME, WHAT DO I DO WHEN GOD BURSTS THAT BUBBLE?
I COME OUT AND BE WHO HE'S CALLED ME TO BE.

LEAVE WHAT OTHER PEOPLE THINK UP TO THEM.
RISE AND SHINE, YOUNG LADY, NOT FOR YOUR OWN GLORY BUT GOD'S.
HE HAS MADE ME WHO I AM
AND I CAN'T WAIT TO SEE WHAT MORE
HE HAS IN STORE.

Reflection 23

THIS POEM CAN BE LOOKED AT OR INTERPRETED IN MANY DIFFERENT WAYS. OUR PERCEPTION ABOUT SITUATIONS OR PEOPLE WHETHER THEY ARE WHITE, BLACK, FAT, SKINNY, TALL, SHORT, LOUD OR QUIET IS JUST THAT—OUR PERCEPTION. IT DOESN'T MEAN, "IT IS WHAT IT IS." IT IS NOT A MATTER OF FACT. PERCEPTION IS NEITHER BLACK NOR WHITE; THERE ARE SHADES OF GRAY.

WE STEREOTYPE RACES AND MANY OTHER THINGS. THERE'S A POPULAR SAYING, "DON'T JUDGE A BOOK BY ITS COVER," BUT IF WE ARE HONEST, AT SOME POINT WE HAVE ALL PREJUDGED A PERSON OR THING UNTIL WE CAME TO THE KNOWLEDGE OF THE TRUTH. THESE THINGS, PEOPLE, AND MAYBE EVEN WE OURSELVES AT ONE POINT HAVE BEEN OR WILL BE MISUNDERSTOOD.

MISUNDERSTOOD

I MAY NOT ALWAYS KNOW WHAT TO DO.
PLEASE DON'T LOOK AT ME LIKE I'M SUPPOSED TO.
SOMETIMES, I DON'T SPEAK MY MIND,
BUT THAT DOESN'T MEAN I'M BLIND.
IF I DON'T ACT LIKE IT'S ALL GOOD,
DON'T LOOK AT ME AS "HOOD."
NO, I'M JUST MISUNDERSTOOD.

PEOPLE TRY TO PUT ME IN A BOX
FOR THE WAY I TALK
OR CONSIDER ME A FOOL OR A CLOWN.
LAUGH IN MY FACE AND TALK ABOUT ME WHEN I'M DOWN.

LET'S GET IT OUT IN THE OPEN SO WE CAN CLEAR THE AIR.
DON'T WAIT 'TIL I'M GONE, SPEAK WHILE I'M HERE.
ONCE IT'S ALL BEHIND, NO NEED TO PRESS REWIND.
I DON'T THINK WE SHOULD.

EVERY BLACK WOMAN IS NOT ANGRY,
NO, THIS ONE'S MISUNDERSTOOD.
IF THERE'S SOMETHING TO BE SAID, IT WILL BE HEARD,
NOT THROUGH ANOTHER, BUT MY OWN WORD.

A CLOSED MOUTH WON'T GET FED, AT LEAST THAT'S WHAT MY HUSBAND SAID.
SO TELL ME WHAT YOU WANT
IF I CAN DO IT.
I'LL SEE TO IT—
I REALLY WOULD.
I'M NOT TRYING TO SAVE THE WORLD;
I'M MISUNDERSTOOD.

IF YOU FOUND A FRIEND IN ME, YOU FOUND A REAL TREASURE.
IT'S NOT JUST FOR NOW, IT'S FOREVER.

I'M SOMETIMES NAIVE SO WITH ME YOU THINK YOU CAN GET OVER
AND AT TIMES YOU WOULD,
BUT GUESS WHAT? ALL THINGS WORK TOGETHER FOR MY GOOD.
MY SILENCE TAKEN FOR WEAKNESS.
I AM WHO I AM, AKA JUST MISUNDERSTOOD.

Made in the USA
Middletown, DE
12 April 2020